A Life Redeemed

From Poverty, Pain, and Human

Trafficking to Faith,

Freedom, and Purpose

Dr. Lende Click

A Life Redeemed

From Poverty, Pain, and Human Trafficking to Faith, Freedom, and Purpose

Table of Contents

Dedication

To my Lord and Savior, Jesus Christ,
who carried me through every valley and never let me go.

To my mother,
whose strength and sacrifice shaped my life.

To my husband, Monroe,
my partner in faith and ministry, walking with me in God's purpose.

And to every person who feels broken, forgotten, or lost—this story is for you.

Author's Note

This book is my testimony of God's faithfulness through poverty, hardship, trauma, healing, and redemption. Every chapter of my life carries evidence that Jesus Christ never left me, never forgot me, never forsook me, and never stopped working in my story.

My prayer is that as you read these pages, you will see that no suffering is wasted when it is placed in God's hands. If God helped me, He can help you too.

Chapter 1

A Child of Grace

I was born in Cebu, Philippines, into a life of deep poverty. We lived in a squatter area—one of the poorest places in the city. Our home was small, our resources were few, and life was not easy.

But even as a little child, I remember something that did not match my circumstances.

I had peace. I had joy.

Even before I fully knew who God was, somewhere deep inside me, I felt that I was not alone.

My father passed away when I was only two years old. From that moment, my mother carried everything on her own.

She worked as a maid for a wealthy family, doing everything she could just to survive and provide. Because of her work, she had to leave me with my cousins.

They were much older than me—ten to fifteen years older.

One of them was very cruel. She was physically abusive. She spoke harsh, painful words. There were days she would eat in front of me and refuse to give me food.

I remember being hungry—so hungry that I would go to a neighbor's house and ask for something to eat. There was a kind older woman who would sometimes give me food. Even now, I remember her kindness. In the middle of hardship, God was already placing people in my life to help me survive.

Despite everything, my mother never stopped trying to give me a better future.

The family she worked for helped sponsor a Catholic private school. Through them, my mother asked if I could study there.

There was only one condition: I had to live at the school, like the orphan children.

Even though I was not an orphan, I had to live as one.

I still remember the day my mother left me there. I cried so hard. My heart broke as she walked away, and I did not understand why I had to stay. I was only six years old.

Life inside the school was very different.

For the first time, I ate meals using utensils. For the first time, I slept in a real bed. I even remember falling off the bed one night because I was not used to it.

It was a new world, but it was not easy.

Some of the older children bullied me. They would give me their food because they were afraid of being punished if they did not finish it. I was too scared to say no, so I ate everything. I remember one day feeling so full that I could barely walk. Even now, I can smile at that memory—a little girl, once hungry, now overwhelmed by too much food.

Our days started early—around five in the morning. We would wake up, eat breakfast together, bathe, and prepare for school. Even though I lived in the orphanage, I was attending one of the most expensive private schools in Cebu. God was already opening doors that I could never open on my own.

I also had something very special—an American couple who sponsored me. They gave me ten dollars. At that time, that was a lot of money. Even as a child, I felt that someone far away cared about me.

But my body was often weak. I was a sick child. I had asthma, and there were times when I became very ill.

One day, I became so sick that I remember going to the bathroom and seeing blood when I urinated. It was a kidney stone problem. The doctors were considering surgery.

My mother was afraid. She told me that when I was young, she worried I might not live long. She prayed to God that I would survive, that I would grow, and that I would walk into my future.

And God heard her prayers.

I did not need surgery. I do not remember everything—only that somehow, I was healed. It was not just medicine. It was mercy.

Because of my condition, my mother decided to take me out of the private school.

I returned to a different life—a public school called City Central School.

This was the reality I knew.

I walked to school wearing flip-flops. There was no bus. No comfort.

Sometimes, I did not even have a bag. I carried my books in my hands or in an old plastic bag, if I could find one.

I had no allowance. Even in grade 1, after school, I already had my own little business. I sold newspapers, and on the weekends, I sold plastic bags in the market. From a very young age, I learned how to work, save, and help my mother however I could.

But I kept going.

Even in poverty, even in pain, even in sickness, God was already writing my story.

A story of survival. A story of grace. A story that was only beginning.

Chapter 2

Strength in the Struggle

After leaving private school, I continued my education at City Central School, a public school in Cebu.

There were no uniforms there, unlike the private school. Life felt more like the world I came from—simple, hard, real.

My mother did everything she could for me.

She had not finished school herself, but she believed deeply in education. She would always tell me that going to school was good for me.

And I believed her.

I loved school.

Even when I was sick, even when I had a fever, I still went. Because I did not want to miss a lesson. I did not want to fall behind. I did not want a bad grade.

We had very little. I had no allowance, but I learned how to save every coin I could find.

My mother never told me I was pretty, but she always told me I was smart. So, I grew up believing I was intelligent, but not beautiful.

Even later in life, when people would tell me I was pretty, I did not believe them.

But God, in His grace, opened my eyes. He showed me that I am beautiful because I am created in His image, and God is beautiful.

In school, something unexpected happened.

Even though I was just a student, I became a helper to my teacher. When we took tests, the teacher checked my paper first. If I made mistakes, she corrected them. Then she would give me the stack of my classmates' papers, and I would grade them.

She even trusted me with a red pen. I corrected papers. I helped prepare report cards. I was still in sixth grade, but I was already carrying responsibility.

Perhaps she saw something in me. Perhaps she believed in me.

Our classrooms were full, sometimes around thirty students in one room. It was crowded. It was noisy. But I stayed focused.

My body was still weak. I could not run or play like the other children. If I tried, I would get sick or struggle to breathe. So instead of playing with kids my age, I spent time with older people. They would listen when I spoke, and they would tell me I had an old soul.

At that time, I did not understand what that meant. But now I do.

God was shaping something deeper inside me.

There were many days I went to school with no food. I would watch my classmates eat while I had nothing. So I learned how to survive. If a classmate did not have homework, they would want to copy mine, and I would let them—in exchange for food or small help.

Even as a child, I was learning how to provide for myself.

But even in those struggles, God was protecting me.

I remember one night, playing near a bakery with other children. There were lights in that area, but beyond it was darkness. A man stood hidden in the shadows. He called my name and asked me to come to him.

For the first time in my life, I felt fear. Something inside me said no. He asked another child to bring me to him, but I refused.

The next day, I found out who he was. He was a rapist. He had hurt other children.

That moment, I knew God had protected me.

Even as a young girl, I talked to God. I did not fully understand Him yet, but I knew He was there.

I remember hiding under a table, looking up at the moon. Wherever I moved, the moon seemed to follow me. I did not understand it then, but in my heart, I felt like I was not alone.

There was another moment I will never forget.

One night, I woke up and told my mother and aunt there was a fire. They thought I was dreaming and told me to go back to sleep.

But I was not dreaming.

Soon after, our entire neighborhood burned to ashes.

Everything was gone.

My mother and I slept outside on cardboard in the streets. And the next day, I still went to school.

With no bag. With nothing.

But I went.

Looking back now, I see something I did not fully understand then.

God was always there protecting me, guiding me, speaking to me, even in ways I could not explain.

A Voice That Refused to Be Silent

My childhood was not marked by abundance, but by survival.

We were poor—so poor that some days it felt as if the world had forgotten us.

But my mother and I refused to be forgotten.

I can still see us standing in the marketplace, selling fruit under the hot sun, with the noise of the busy streets all around us.

She worked hard, and so did I, because there was no other choice.

Even then, I carried a strange kind of hope. I believed there was a bigger picture for my life. I could not see it yet. I did not fully know Jesus. But deep in my soul, I talked to Him as if He were close. Somehow, I knew He was not far away.

Poverty tried to silence me, but I learned early to use my voice.

At Christmas time, while many focused on what they lacked, I gathered my friends. We went from place to place, singing carols. I even made my own instrument—flattened bottle caps nailed into wood, shaking them like bells. We made joyful noise, and people gave us food. Sometimes even chicken— something we only had on very special days.

I was always the leader.

We did not just sing. We brought lights.

I also learned how to work.

At just seven years old, I began selling newspapers. I would buy them for twenty-five cents and sell them for thirty-five. Ten cents profit. Little by little, I grew.

Sometimes people gave me extra out of kindness, and I was so happy. I gave what I earned to my mother. She never forced me. I just knew this was what I needed to do.

On weekends, I sell plastic bags in the market.

During Christmas and New Year, my mother trusted me with capital for business. I bought apples by the box and sold them one by one. I sold New Year noisemakers and seasonal items, and I made good profit.

Even as a young girl, I was learning business.

I gave everything back to my mother, and we used it not only for ourselves but also to help others. My mother taught me something I would never forget: always give back.

There were times I saved just to buy simple things, like shoes.

When I entered high school at Abellana National School, I wanted something simple—a pair of rubber shoes, not flipflops, just like the other students.

School was still my priority. Even when life was hard, I did not give up.

Some students had money, food, and support. I had none of those things, but I had determination, and I had faith.

Looking back now, those moments were not just survival. They were training.

God was teaching me leadership, faith, perseverance, wisdom, and provision—even when I did not fully understand it.

Chapter 3

The Day I Found Him

During my high school years, life was still very hard.

We lived in a small, rented room—just one room—for four people: my mother, my uncle, my "big sister," and me. Four people. One room. Sleeping on the floor.

That was our life.

One night, a fire broke out. It started near a store that sold oxygen tanks. The flames spread quickly. The fire blocked the main path. There was no way out.

We were trapped.

But in that moment, I heard something—not with my ears alone, but deep inside me. A voice.

Clear. Strong.

Go to the other room. Tell them to open the wall.

I told the others that we had to go that way. At first, they did not understand. But when we went to that room, they discovered a hidden window.

We got out. We survived.

My uncle cried. He thought we were all going to die.

But God made a way.

Then came the day that changed everything.

June 12, 1981.

I was thirteen years old.

That was the day I gave my life to Jesus Christ.

Before that, I grew up going to church. We prayed. We followed rituals, sometimes even in a language I did not understand. It was Latin. But something was missing.

Around that time, my aunt came back from Canada. She was very sick. Doctors said she only had six months to live. Her own children did not take care of her, but my mother did. So, she came to live with us.

One day, a neighbor told us about a healing service. We went. It was held underground in Santo Rosario.

I remember seeing a priest, but he did not look like a priest. He wore jeans and a T-shirt.

For the first time in my life, I heard the truth clearly:

Jesus is the mediator between God and man. Jesus is the one who died for me. Through Him, I receive eternal life.

I had never heard that before, not like that, not so personal.

Then he said that if anyone wanted to accept Jesus, they should come forward.

There was no altar. Just, a space.

I did not ask my mother. I did not hesitate. I just walked forward, and in my heart, I said that I accepted Jesus as my Lord and Savior.

And then something happened.

I felt heat, like fire, but it did not burn. It started in my head and moved through my whole body.

I can still remember it.

When I went home, I did not know how to pray. So, I just spoke from my heart. I told God He was a good God, the King of kings, the Lord of lords, the Master of the universe, and that I loved Him.

Then came the dreams.

I dreamed of Him.

First, I saw Him as a baby, surrounded by light so bright yet gentle it did not hurt my eyes.

Then I saw Him on the cross. I could see His form but not His face, only bright light.

Then I saw Him ascending into heaven, wearing a white robe, rising into glory.

I told my mother. She listened and smiled.

From that moment, I knew—not just in my mind, but in my heart—that God is real.

Before, I talked to Him like He was far away. Now I talked to Him like He was right there with me, because He was.

Even in poverty, even in hardship, I was never empty, because I had something deeper than happiness. I had joy.

That day—June 12, 1981—was not just a moment.

It was the beginning of a new life.

Chapter 4

A Faith That Would Not Be Stopped

After I gave my life to Jesus, something inside me began to change.

I refused to let poverty decide who I would become.

I went to school not because I was the smartest, not because I was the most privileged, but because I believed there was more. A bigger picture. A higher calling. A God who saw me even when others overlooked me.

Inside, I carried a constant conversation with Him. Even before I fully understood everything, I knew He was real. I spoke to Him like He was right in front of me.

I had never read the Bible. Growing up, I was told that only the priest could read it. But deep inside, I always said that when I grew up, I wanted a Bible.

And one day, my mother bought me one—a small Bible from a Protestant store. I still have it today, along with the songbook she gave me. That was in 1981.

That year, I learned something that would stay with me forever: faith can live in the cracks of hardship, even when everything around you looks small and broken.

That seed of faith inside me never stopped growing.

As I began to share about Jesus, I faced rejection—even from my own family. My cousins did not want to hear it. They preferred rituals and religion.

But I told them that God wants a relationship with us.

They did not understand. They did not listen.

But even then, I knew I had a calling, to tell people the Good News.

When I was younger, I used to ask God why I could not sing like others or dance like them. I thought I had no special gifts. But as I grew older, I realized God had already given me gifts— the ones I needed: wisdom, understanding, and hunger for Him.

There were things I did not fully understand yet. People would tell me strange things, like not to read the Bible because it would make me crazy. But deep inside, I knew that was not true.

Even when I did not have everything, I had Him. And that was enough.

But life was not without storms. After my salvation, the challenges did not stop. In fact, a greater storm was coming.

When I was in my fourth year of high school, something unexpected happened. A neighbor came to our home and told my mother that her daughter was living in Germany, married to a German man, and that others were going there too.

When I heard that, something stirred inside me.

I wanted to go too.

My mother hesitated because I had not finished school yet. But the opportunity was there. They offered to take care of everything—my papers and my passport. We did not need to pay anything.

I told my teacher I would be leaving. There was one teacher I will never forget, Sir Ernesto Jacel, my Algebra teacher. He saw something in me, and his belief stayed with me, especially in moments when life felt impossible.

I left during Christmas break. I missed months of school, but because I had good grades, I was still able to pass.

There was one teacher who wanted to fail me. She was my Home Economics teacher, and she wanted to fail me because I did not have my project. I was not there anymore, because I had already left. If I failed, I would not graduate.

But God made a way.

I left for Germany, not fully understanding what was ahead, but trusting that God was leading me.

Chapter 5

Through the Fire, Not Consumed

I thought I was going to Germany to work. I believed it was an opportunity—a way to help my family, a step into a better future.

But when I arrived, everything changed.

At the airport, I saw a man. He was big—very big. And I was small, not even ninety pounds.

They took my passport and handed me over to him.

I said I did not want to go with him, but they told me that I had to.

He brought me to his home. I stayed there for two weeks—crying and praying, crying and praying.

Later, I learned the truth.

I had been sold into human trafficking.

Fifteen thousand Deutsche Marks.

I was only sixteen years old.

They brought me back to the place where other girls were. Some were hurt. Some were violated. Some became pregnant. But by the grace of God, no one touched me.

There was another girl there—her name was Femmie. She had also been sold. She already knew.

I began to understand what had been done to us. This was not help. This was not opportunity. This was deception.

They tried to give me to a man. He was forty-nine years old. Tall. Strong. To me, he looked like a giant.

What hurt the most was not just fear. It was, the reality that I had been treated like something to be bought.

They bargained over me as if I were standing in a marketplace.

But God was still writing my story.

They found another man. His name was Peter. He was shy. His mother had bought a wife for him—bought me.

But I knew this was not my life.

Before I ran away, I asked for my passport. I told them I needed it for paperwork, and they gave it to me.

I slept with my clothes on, ready.

Then I ran.

I called my mother and told her I wanted to come home, but she told me that I was already there and should stay.

So, I stayed—but not in that place, not in that life.

I found work.

My first job was washing dishes. The pots were bigger than me. I had to stand on a stool just to reach.

Then I found another job in a factory assembling parts for VHS video machines.

I worked hard. Faithfully.

But there was still fear that I could be deported.

Then something happened. A coworker named Karen saw me and said she wanted to help me. She cared enough to say that if she could, she would even adopt me so I could stay.

The owner of the company wrote a letter to the German government, saying that I was a good worker and that they would help me stay.

God made a way again.

Life did not suddenly become easy. There were still struggles, tears, and long nights.

But something inside me had changed.

I was no longer just surviving.

Resilience became my nature. Faith became my foundation.

Every small victory was proof that God was shaping me.

I remembered everything I had learned—selling fruit, saving every coin, multiplying what little I had, even the twenty dollars my mother gave me before I left for Germany, the only money she had.

People began to see me not just as a poor girl from the market, but as someone with vision, courage, and determination.

What they did not see were the tears, the prayers whispered in the dark, and the nights I almost gave up.

But I carried those things proudly, because they were proof that I was climbing.

My story was never just about me.

It was always about God.

Chapter 6

Rising to Higher Ground

People began to see me differently.

No longer just a poor girl from the market, but someone with vision, courage, and determination.

What they did not see were the long nights, the tears, and the prayers whispered in the dark.

I carried those costs quietly and proudly, because they were proof that I was climbing.

The climb was never easy. There were setbacks, battles, and moments I wanted to stop. But every time I stumbled, I remembered I was not walking alone.

My story was never just about me. It was about God—His strength revealed through my weakness.

Step by step, He brought me to higher ground.

Looking back, I do not just see hardship. I see a path that shaped my faith.

Poverty tried to define me, but resilience gave me a new name. Struggle tried to silence me, but my voice found strength in songs, in prayers, and in hope.

I remembered the fruit market, the Christmas carols, and the twenty dollars my mother gave me, which became more than money.

These are not just memories. They are testimonies.

I have learned that resilience is not the absence of pain. It is the decision to keep going, to trust, and to believe when everything around me says otherwise.

True strength is not found in what we hold, but in who holds us.

And I know without a doubt that my Lord and Savior Jesus Christ has carried me every step of the way.

If my story says anything, let it say this: you are never too poor, too broken, or too forgotten for God to use you.

What looks small in your hands can become great in His. What feels like an ending can become the beginning of your testimony.

I am living proof that resilience through hardship is possible—not by my power, but by His grace.

And this was only the beginning.

Life began to stabilize. I was able to stay in Germany. I worked. I stood on my own.

And then I met my first husband.

His name was Joel. He was only a year and a half older than I was.

I was nineteen years old, and to me he was very handsome.

I remember asking him why he liked me because I did not think I was pretty. He told me I was pretty, but I did not believe him.

I prayed to God that if it was His will, Joel would become my husband.

One day, I had a dream that he would leave Germany and return to America. Not long after, it happened. Because of his work in the military, he had to go back.

We continued our relationship, even with the distance.

Then in November 1989, we were married.

Shortly after, I went with him to America.

When I met his mother, she said something that hurt me deeply. She told me that if I had been darker, she would not have allowed me into her home.

That moment stayed with me. But even then, God was still with me.

Joel was stationed at Fort Carson in Colorado Springs, and that is where my life in America began.

Soon after, I became pregnant. I did not know it at first. Then one day I became very sick and began to bleed.

We went to the emergency room, and that is when I found out I was pregnant.

The doctors said I might lose the baby.

But I prayed. I rested. I trusted God.

And my son was born.

Joshua Noah, born on July 25, 1991.

Later that same year, another door opened.

I became a United States citizen.

From a little girl in the marketplace to a woman standing in a new nation—only God could write a story like that.

Chapter 7

Love, Loss, and a Mother's Sacrifice

At the beginning of our marriage, I was happy.

He was kind to me. He cared for me. In my eyes, he was very handsome.

But slowly, things began to change.

I remember one moment clearly. I had written a check to buy clothes for our children—something simple, something necessary.

He became upset.

That was the first time, and from there, little by little, hurtful things began to grow.

I was pregnant with our second child, and the man I once admired was becoming someone I did not recognize.

Women would flirt with him in public, and sometimes he would flirt back.

That hurt deeply, because to me he was not just my husband. He was supposed to be my best friend.

Our second child, Jodelen, was born on June 30, 1993, in Kaiserslautern, Germany.

I stayed home at first. I became a mother. I babysat other children to help support our family, and later I worked as a manager.

But I began to notice something troubling: my money was "our money," but his money was "his money." He made investments, but only in his name, and I did not know until later.

Then came something even more painful.

He had an affair.

There were signs. Things that did not make sense. He would leave early even when he did not need to. Phone calls would come and hang up when I answered, but not when he did.

One day, I invited the woman into our home. I cooked for them. From the kitchen, I could hear them laughing, but when I walked into the room, they became quiet.

There were times I would pick him up from work. From outside, I could see inside the building. They could not see me, but I could see them—standing close together, talking closely.

When I walked in, they separated.

The truth was there, even if no one said it.

Eventually, I made a decision.

I asked for a divorce.

I was given custody of my children in Germany, but the battle was not over.

Chapter 8

Carried Through the Valley

When I was twenty-six years old, God gave me a dream.

In the dream, I was driving a long gray Ford LTD. The car was so big, and I was so small. I had to sit on pillows—one behind my back and one beneath me—just to see the road.

The road was narrow. The buildings around me were tall, and everything was filled with bright light.

I remember saying to myself that I was going home.

Then something happened.

I drove toward a house, but it was not like a normal house. It felt like another dimension.

My car did not go inside, but suddenly I was inside.

Then I saw myself standing there.

And then I saw myself rising—higher and higher—until I stopped.

Then someone came toward me wearing a long robe. I could not see His face.

But as He came closer, I saw who He was carrying.

It was me.

He was carrying me.

I woke up suddenly and prayed that the Lord would not take me yet because my children were still so young. Joshua was not even four. Jodelen was not even two.

I did not understand the dream, so I prayed and asked God what it meant.

The answer came: I was about to go through a tribulation—a time when I would not be able to stand, not be able to walk, and He would be the one to carry me.

Just a few days later, it happened.

He took my children and brought them to America, to Athens, Georgia.

And I was left alone in a country where I had no family and no support.

But God still made a way.

A friend helped me. Her mother-in-law allowed me to stay with her. That kindness I will never forget.

Then came the court.

I stood there alone.

He stood there with his whole family.

The judge said he would be given temporary custody because I lived in Germany and he lived in America.

I said that I already had permanent custody in Germany.

But the judge replied that this was not Germany, this was America.

Those words broke my heart.

In that moment, I faced a decision.

I could fight and risk losing everything, or I could sacrifice.

And I chose sacrifice.

I told him that I would not divorce him.

And for ten years, I stayed.

Ten years of my life, given up so that my children would remember me, so that I could stay in their lives.

Because I knew that if I walked away completely, they might forget me.

And that, I could not bear it.

But even in that pain, God was there.

The same God I talked to as a child in the marketplace was still with me. In the silence, in the shadows, and in the broken places, I whispered to Him.

His presence became my strength.

I will not pretend it was easy. There was fear, darkness, and deep pain.

But there was also faith.

I learned that resilience is not the absence of suffering. It is surviving suffering with faith.

Those years could have destroyed me, my heart, my faith, my identity.

But instead, they formed me.

Yes, I carried scars, but I also carried strength.

The same God who protected me at sixteen when I was sold into human trafficking was the same God who carried me now.

Different tribulation. Same God.

I cried. I worked. I kept going, even when I had to hide my tears behind sunglasses.

Because life did not stop, and neither could I.

Through it all, I held onto this truth: I do not look at how big the problem is. I look at how big my God is.

And now, when I look back, I know He carried me all the way through.

Chapter 9

Set Free, Made Whole

I want to say something clearly.

I did not hate Joel.

One day, with tears in my eyes, I told him that he could have everything—the house and even the children—but that he needed to let me go and set me free.

I did not want to fight. I did not want to go through long court battles. My heart wanted peace.

I just wanted a clean divorce.

And finally, he agreed.

He said I could have the children. He would not fight me.

We went to the lawyer, and that was the beginning of my healing.

For so long, I had not been able to go to church freely. If I went to church, he would become angry. Even when I invited him to come with me, he refused.

There were times it felt like war in the house just because I wanted to worship God.

But I never stopped praying. I never stopped reading my Bible.

And when I was finally free, I ran to God.

I began going to Fleming Baptist Church, and I stayed there for sixteen years. I started in 2006.

For the first time in a long time, I felt peace. I felt joy. I felt freedom.

At the same time, I was working hard.

I had already started building something of my own—a business.

I sold children's toys, sunglasses, handbags, and scrub uniforms.

Before that, I even had a clothing store, but I moved to the flea market because the rent was more affordable.

During the week, I worked at Blockbuster, a video rental store. I was a manager. I worked Monday to Thursday so I could have insurance for myself. My children had military benefits, but I did not.

Then on Friday, Saturday, and Sunday, I worked at the flea market.

I worked long hours. I did whatever I had to do—not just to survive, but to rebuild my life.

I remember looking at pictures of myself during my marriage. I looked tired—older than I should have been. Stress had marked my face. My body carried the weight.

But now, I was changing.

Healing had begun.

The scars were still there, but they were no longer open wounds.

They were healing.

When I looked back on my life, I saw something clearly: God's hand had always been on me.

Even when I was sold at sixteen, He was there.

Even when I lost my children, He was there.

Even when I felt broken, He was there.

He gave me strength when I had none. He gave me courage when I wanted to give up.

Those chapters left scars, but they also gave me a testimony.

I was taken as a young girl, but I was not destroyed, because no one can steal the faith that God planted deep inside my soul.

When my children were taken, it broke me, but it did not finish me, because resilience was still there. Faith was still there.

I am who I am today because of what I went through.

Just like gold must go through fire to be refined, so did I.

And through that fire, I was not destroyed. I was formed.

I learned to forgive.

I forgave Joel. I forgave those who hurt me. Even those who sold me.

And then justice came.

The people who sold me went to jail.

I stood in court. I testified. I told the truth.

And they were held accountable.

My story was even written about. I was in the newspaper twice. They called me a runaway bride.

But I knew the truth.

I was not running away.

I was being set free.

And everything I went through, every tribulation, became my testimony.

Because it is by the word of our testimony that we overcome.

And I became an overcomer.

Chapter 10

From Darkness to Destiny

When I was sixteen years old, my freedom was stolen.

I was sold into human trafficking.

Before that, I thought I knew hardship—poverty, hunger, and long days in the market.

But nothing could have prepared me for the moment I realized I had been sold.

I did not even know the words *human trafficking*. All I knew was that I was living, a nightmare.

I was taken to Germany. Everything felt unfamiliar—the language, the faces, the streets.

But the greatest fear was not being in a foreign place.

It was this: I had no voice, no choice, no value.

At sixteen, I should have been dreaming about my future.

Instead, I was fighting just to survive each day.

But even in that darkness, I held onto a truth I had learned as a child: I was not alone.

In my pain, I whispered that I did not understand why this was happening and that I did not know how to escape, but I believed God was near and that He heard me.

The world told me I was forgotten, but deep inside I knew my Savior, Jesus Christ, had not abandoned me.

The days were heavy. The nights were even heavier.

Fear tried to silence me. Shame tried to chain me.

But I found my strength in prayer.

Resilience was no longer just about working hard or multiplying a few dollars.

It became surviving the unthinkable.

Looking back now, I see clearly: God's hand was upon me even then.

He gave me strength when I had none. He gave me courage when I wanted to give up.

Yes, that chapter left scars.

But it also gave me a testimony.

I was taken, but I was not broken.

That sixteen-year-old girl learned something powerful: no one can steal the faith planted deep inside my soul.

When I finally walked out of that darkness, I was not the same girl.

I was wounded. I was scared.

But I was also strong, because God had carried me through the valley of shadows.

Healing did not happen overnight. Trauma does not disappear quietly.

There were nights when memories returned and days when fear tried to follow me.

But step by step, prayer by prayer, I began to take myself back.

And I learned something profound: resilience is not pretending pain never happened. It is looking at the scars and saying, "This is not where my story ends."

My faith grew deeper. My voice grew stronger.

What the enemy meant to destroy me, God was already turning into a testimony.

And slowly, I began to find joy again.

I realized my life still had purpose—a bigger picture, just like I believed when I was a child.

The same God I spoke to in the marketplace, the same Savior who was near in Germany, was still guiding me forward.

After surviving the unthinkable, I knew one thing: my life could never stay the same.

I had walked through a storm that should have destroyed me, and yet I was still standing, still breathing, still believing.

Because my victory was not in my strength. It was in Christ Jesus.

And God was not finished with me.

Chapter 11

Called to the Light

On April 21, 2008, a Monday, God gave me another dream.

In the dream, I saw myself, but not as I was on earth. I saw myself on the other side.

There was a place filled with light. Not a light that hurts your eyes, but a bright, pure, peaceful light.

There were only a few people there. They were wearing white robes.

And I noticed that they were standing in line.

They were waiting for a door.

And that door was brighter than anything else.

I was watching them, and suddenly they turned. They could see me, and I could see them.

Then God showed me something else.

He took me to another place.

This place was completely different.

It was dark—not just dark, but deep, heavy, jet-black darkness.

And I saw people there.

They were naked. They were blind.

I was close enough to see them, but they could not see me.

And I asked the Lord what it meant.

He said that they were blind because they were blinded from the truth, and naked because they had no shame.

Then He reminded me of His Word—the ten virgins in Matthew 25. Five were wise. Five were foolish. The wise had oil in their lamps. The foolish did not.

When the door opened, the wise went in. The foolish were left outside, crying for the Lord to open to them. But He said He did not know them.

Then He showed me more—the wheat and the tares. The wheat goes into the barn, but the tares go into the fire. He also showed me the Word from Revelation that says blessed is the one who watches and keeps his garments, lest he walk naked and they see his shame.

Then the Lord spoke to me.

Tell them.

And I said that I could not because people would think I was crazy.

But He spoke again the next day, and again on the third day.

Finally, I said that if He wanted me to tell them, He had to help me.

And He did.

When I began to share the dream, people gave their lives to Jesus.

That was the beginning.

In May 2008, I started jail ministry.

I went on Sundays. I went on Thursdays.

And even now, many years later, I am still going.

Every time I walk in, I feel the presence of the Holy Spirit—not fear, but His presence.

I tell them there is hope.

I tell them my story.

I was homeless, there is hope.

I was sold into human trafficking—there is hope.

I was abused—there is hope.

My children were taken from me—there is hope.

No matter what you go through, there is hope.

And that hope is Jesus Christ.

I have gone to many places—West Virginia, the Philippines, and Germany—sharing the Good News.

Because I realized something.

My life was never just about survival.

It was about purpose.

Everything I went through was not wasted.

God carried me through the fire for a reason.

Work was no longer just about making a living. It became a mission field. At my job, at the flea market, and everywhere I went, I shared the Good News.

People would ask me how I could still smile, how I could still believe, and how I was still standing.

My answer was simple.

Because I am not alone.

I have never been alone.

My story—from poverty to pain to trauma—became a door to show others the power of faith, the strength of resilience, and the love of God.

God does not rescue us only for ourselves.

He rescues us so we can help rescue others.

That became my calling.

I was not just rebuilding my life.

I was helping others believe they could rebuild theirs too.

Chapter 12

Set Apart

Years passed, and I remained single.

Not because I had no opportunities, but because I had made a decision.

I belonged to Jesus.

My life was no longer my own. My body was not my own. My purpose was not my own.

Many people came into my life. Many asked me out. Some were kind. Some were wealthy. Some were very handsome.

But I was not looking for those things.

I was guarding something far more valuable—my relationship with God.

A married man named Jason approached me and said he wanted to be with me, but I refused because I belonged to Jesus.

I took him aside and told him that he did not respect Jesus, me, or his wife, and that what he was asking was wrong.

That was the end of it.

Others came too—a doctor, a wealthy businessman, men with influence, money, and status.

But my answer was always the same.

No.

Because I knew this truth: my body belongs to Jesus.

I had already been through too much to give away what God had redeemed.

I was not going back.

I saw myself differently now.

I am His bride. I am a warrior for Christ.

And I would not live for the things of this world.

I would live for the Kingdom of God.

Then someone came into my life.

Different. Persistent, but

respectful.

His name is Monroe.

At first, I said no—again and again.

Even when he asked just to talk, just to have coffee, I refused.

But he did not give up easily.

Finally, I agreed to talk. Just conversation.

We sat across from each other, and he kept his word. He respected me.

We talked. We got to know each other. And something began to grow.

Even my daughter noticed. She said he was very lucky because I never gave my number to anyone.

And she was right, because I was careful and did not let people get close to me easily.

I waited. I prayed. Because I had learned never to move without God.

Then one day, I had a dream. In the dream, he gave me a ring.

I told him about it. He laughed.

But a few weeks later, he asked me to be his wife.

And I knew God had spoken.

Because everything in my life—every decision, every step—had to pass through Him.

Even love.

Chapter 13

A Life Restored, A Legacy of Hope

Today, I am no longer alone.

I am married.

Before I married Monroe, he once asked me what I would say if he found someone just like me.

I smiled and said, "Good luck," meaning it would be hard to find someone who truly loves Jesus and follows Him.

And he does.

He is a follower of Jesus.

Together, we serve the Lord.

We both do jail ministry. We both share the Good News. We both go where God sends us.

And we made a decision that we would not take money for preaching or sharing the Gospel. We trust God to provide.

Because this is not our work.

This is His.

For many years, my life was about survival.

But then something changed.

Survival became courage. Courage became action.

I never forgot the faces of those who had sold me. I never forgot the fear, the pain, and the darkness.

But I also never forgot my God — the One who promised that evil would not have the final word.

And one day, justice came.

The very people who trafficked me were brought to court.

I stood there. I testified. I told the truth.

And they were sent to prison.

It was not revenge I wanted.

It was justice.

Justice for the sixteen-year-old girl I once was. Justice for the other girls. Justice so others would not suffer the same fate.

And in that moment, I realized something powerful.

My scars had become my sword.

The pain of my past became the power to protect.

God had turned my deepest valley into a platform for victory.

After the storm, after the fire, and after the justice, I longed for something steady. Something rooted. Something filled with love.

And God gave me that.

Family. Not just by blood, but by faith. My brothers and sisters in Christ. My community. My calling.

I built my life on what I learned. I knew what it was to be poor, so I became grateful. I knew what it was to be silenced, so I gave others a voice. I knew what it was to be broken, so I helped others heal.

My life was not about perfection.

It was about resilience.

It was about showing up, loving others, and living out my faith daily.

I had been a child in the marketplace, a girl trafficked across countries, and a young woman standing in court.

But now, I am, something more.

A witness. A vessel. A living testimony.

Every time I tell my story, I see hearts open. I see tears fall. I see hope rise.

Because people realize that if God can lift me out of darkness, He can do the same for them.

Faith is not just words.

It is action.

It is standing for the voiceless, fighting for justice, feeding the hungry, encouraging the broken, and lifting the weak.

It is reminding people that they are not alone.

I have learned that my life is not about what I lost. It is about what God restored.

The pain, the scars, and the battles became seeds.

And when planted in faith, they grew into something greater than I could ever imagine.

My testimony became my weapon, my shield, and my gift.

If my story means anything, let it say this: there is hope.

For the broken. For the forgotten. For the ones who feel unseen.

Because God sees you.

He saw me.

And He never let go.

Final Chapter

A Life Redeemed

When I look back at my childhood, what stands out is not comfort or abundance, but survival.

We were poor, my mother and I, yet poverty never broke our spirit. Instead, it shaped me into the person I became.

When I look back now, I do not just see hardship. I see a story written with tears, but also with triumph. I see valleys deep with pain, but mountaintops crowned with victory.

From the little girl selling fruit in the market, to selling newspapers at seven, to selling plastic bags on the weekends, to building my own business—every chapter became my testimony. A testimony of resilience.

Even the hardest moments carried me closer to truth.

And today, I know this: no suffering is ever wasted when it is placed in God's hands.

This is not the end of my story.

It is the beginning of my legacy.

Because if there is one thing my life has taught me, it is this:

No matter where you begin, with faith, with courage, and with God, you can rise.

I have seen it with my own life.

I was sold into human trafficking, but I was never forgotten.

I was afraid, but I was never destroyed.

I went through pain, trauma, and tears, but I also walked into victory.

Because I was never alone.

Today, I stand as a woman redeemed—not because of my own strength, but because of God, who never let me go.

Today, God has blessed me in ways I never imagined.

I now have my own business, buying and selling homes. This has become my provision, my bread and butter.

But more importantly, I continue in ministry.

I still go to the jails. I still share hope. I still tell the Good News.

God opened another door for me. I went back to school. I earned my doctorate in clinical counseling.

I became a licensed clinical counselor and a Christian counselor so I could help more people and reach more lives—not for my glory, but for His.

Because He is a good God.

If God can help me, He can help you.

No matter what you have been through, there is hope.

God loves you.

That is why Jesus died—for you and for me—so that we may have eternal life with Him.

Jesus loves you. The Father loves you. The Holy Spirit loves you.

If you open your heart to Him, He will come into your life. He will never leave you nor forsake you.

Because His Word is true.

He is real.

He is the God of the universe.

This is my story—a story of resilience, hardship, justice, and redemption.

This is my legacy.

A life redeemed.

And I am redeemed by the blood of Jesus Christ.

Author Bio

Dr. Lende Click is a Christian author, speaker, counselor, and minister whose life story is a powerful testimony of faith, resilience, justice, healing, and redemption.

Born in Cebu, Philippines, and raised in poverty, she overcame unimaginable hardships—including human trafficking, trauma, loss, and adversity—through her unwavering faith in Jesus Christ.

Today, she serves through jail ministry, missions, counseling, speaking, business, and writing, helping others find healing, hope, and purpose. She holds a doctorate in clinical counseling and is passionate about sharing the love of Christ through her life and testimony.

Some proceeds from her work help support children in Cebu, Philippines.

Also by Dr. Lende Click

A Life Redeemed is one of many faith-filled books by Dr. Lende Click, written to encourage hearts, strengthen faith, and point readers to the redeeming love of Jesus Christ.

Other books by Dr. Lende Click include:

The Gift of Godly Friendship
A Bible study for women who long for meaningful, godly connection.

Daughters of the King
An 8-week Bible study workbook for women growing in faith, identity, and purpose.

Prayers of a Daughter of the King
A devotional journey of prayer, strength, and deeper intimacy with God.

God Is Still Writing Your Story
A faith-filled message of hope for those learning to trust God in unfinished seasons.

When God Carries a Woman Through the Fire
A powerful encouragement for women walking through pain, testing, and restoration.

Serving the Lord with a Willing Heart
A 12-Week Bible Study on Faithful Service for the Lord

Healing for the Woman Who Has Been Hurt
A Bible Study for Finding Hope, Restoration, and Wholeness in Christ

Faith & Courage Children's Books

Sammy the Shy Snail's Big Race
A gentle story of courage, faith, and believing God can help you do hard things.

Bella the Brave Butterfly and the Stormy Day
A sweet story teaching children courage and trust in God during fearful times.

Toby the Turtle Who Trusted God
A faith-filled story about learning to trust God one step at a time.

Delen's Story: Faith Like Sunshine
An uplifting story of faith, hope, and God's light shining through every season.

Christian Fantasy

The Kingdom of Everlight
An epic faith-filled fantasy story of courage, destiny, and the triumph of light over darkness.

The Kingdom of Everlight: The Crown of Hidden Fire
An Epic Christian Fantasy of Courage, Sacrifice, and the Light That Darkness Cannot Destroy

Thank you for supporting books that share faith, courage, healing, and hope.

Some proceeds from my books help support children in Cebu, Philippines, through children's ministry.